YOUNG Divas
THAT CARE

YOUNG Divas THAT CARE

COMPILED BY
CANDACE GISH

bhc press

Livonia, Michigan

Edited by Lana King

YOUNG DIVAS THAT CARE
Copyright © 2020 Candace Gish
All rights reserved. Except as permitted under the U.S. Copyright Act of 1976, no part of this publication may be reproduced, distributed, or transmitted in any form or by any means, or stored in a database or retrieval system, without prior written permission of the publisher.

Published by BHC Press

Library of Congress Control Number: 2019948351

ISBN: 978-1-64397-052-3 (Softcover)
ISBN: 978-1-64397-053-0 (Ebook)

For information, write:
BHC Press
885 Penniman #5505
Plymouth, MI 48170

Visit the publisher:
www.bhcpress.com

TABLE OF CONTENTS

15
ARAYA HOWARD

23
MELISSA SMITH

33
NATASHA PANDUWAWALA

41
MEGAN LOH

47
MAHEALANI SIMS-TULBA

53
RILEY CALLEN

59
DANIKA GORDON

65
MADELENE KLEINHANS

71
AMBER NELSON

77
LUCILLE JOHNSTONE

81
MEAGAN WARREN

87
ABBY DIUBLE

**95
ZOYA SURANI**

**101
DANIELLE ROTHCHILD**

**107
JOCELYN MARENCIK**

**111
LIBBY HAWBOLDT**

**119
CALLA LEGUE**

This book is dedicated to my
four amazing Diva Daughters
who inspire me each and every day
to be a Changemaker.

Also to all the extraordinary young women
in this world that are about to tap
into their greatness so they can
live their lives to the fullest.

So, what does DIVAS stand for?

A woman who is *Determined* to reach her goals.

Individuals who celebrate their uniqueness.

Those who are *Victorious* in conquering their fears.

Someone who is *Always* ready to speak out about things that are important to them.

Someone who others are able to rely on.

AN INTRODUCTION

The need for this powerful series of anthologies was revealed to creator Candace Gish while vacationing. She couldn't help but feel uneasy when she noticed the vast differences between the haves and the have-nots in our world.

Candace returned home from her trip ignited and hungry to leverage the platforms of her business and radio show to help bridge that glaring gap.

In her search for inspiration and support to bring forth change, Candace was disappointed to find that she would face far more dead ends than she anticipated.

So, like any good entrepreneur with no time to wait for a seat at the table, she decided to create a table for herself.

The vision for the Young Divas That Care anthology is to create a community of committed women. They pride themselves as women whose ideas and strategies on how collaborative efforts to make our world a better place are coined not only for themselves but also for future generations.

Welcome to the movement of Divas That Care!
Change begins with us.

YOUNG Divas THAT CARE

ARAYA HOWARD
Mental Health Advocate,
Poet

ABOUT ARAYA HOWARD

Araya Howard is an eighteen-year-old mental health advocate who uses her platform to speak about her experiences with body image and bullying. She volunteers in schools around her city teaching children about mental health stigma, bullying, and how what we say has an impact on others.

It's hard to find the empowerment we need
in order to live our own lives

Empowerment comes from yourself,
it comes from the communities we're in
but we often forget that it even exists

We need to stop and ask ourselves
Who we are surrounding ourselves with
and if they make us happy

Finding empowerment starts with finding
role models, finding people who
you can look up to

Finding people with similar or
different opinions and ideas

Find people who make you feel confident
Find empowerment in other females
Find the empowerment in yourself
to even just exist

Find people who inspire you to be you
Women supporting women is magical

When you have the support of
Other women who have broken through the hold
of society you start to feel inspired

You feel inspired to change, you feel inspired to be
your best version of you

Empowerment and confidence play a
large part in finding yourself
A confident women is a strong woman
All women are strong women

Finding confidence doesn't happen overnight

Confidence is self love.
Self love is loving yourself so much that words
and opinions can't hurt you

We females are strong, we tolerate aggressive
behavior and taunts just about every day
Find empowerment in the fact that you have
survived and will continue to do so

Surround yourself with as much positivity
as you can, find new groups of people,
give someone a compliment

People are hurting as much as you might be that
compliment might just mean the world to them

When you find the freedom to be yourself
you are finally yourself

When you find people who support you to the
fullest extent that they can you will feel free
You will feel like nothing will ever
be able to hurt you

YOUNG DIVAS THAT CARE

Inspiration will come to you
It will hit you in waves everything will
look better once you feel free
Once you feel supported

You do not have to battle through the world alone
You don't have to fight by yourself

Find your community
Find your inspiration in them, in yourself
Find your confidence and live
your life to the fullest
Don't worry about society or the people
who want to hold you down

Support your fellow women and
they will support you back

    I grew up believing society's rules on what I should and shouldn't wear, who I could and couldn't be, what I should do to be a proper woman, etc. As kids we tend to believe everything we're told because we're innocent and naïve. A young girl being told that she can't play sports because she's weak happens way too often. Too often girls are underestimated/not given a chance because they are female. Luckily, I was raised by two parents who did not force me to follow the stereotypical gender roles that are forced upon us at a young age. They put me in dance and in soccer, and I like to think I was great at both.
    As a little girl growing up, I always had to prove myself to the boys while playing soccer during recess. I worked fifteen times harder to be picked for the teams, to be passed the ball. I was taunted for not only being fat and playing soccer (the funny joke of a fat kid running

for something other than food was absolutely never overused, and if you can't tell, I'm being sarcastic) but also for being female and trying to play soccer with the boys. Trying to prove myself also meant bruises and broken glasses all of which I was proud of. Teachers were especially worried that I'd be hurt because "boys are boys, and they like to push and shove." I mean, technically though that was soccer. You get pushed over or shoved to the ground so that the opponent can grab the ball and try to score, but you pick yourself up off the ground (even if you're hurt or exhausted) and keep playing and running to try to catch up. In essence, that's what being female is. It's being pushed down, being torn down, being exhausted, hurt, and still trying. Still trying to get out of the gender roles and stereotypes that follow and surround us our entire lives.

Empowerment for females is still quite hard to find. In all seriousness, there's still very much a women vs. women mentality. It's not taught but learned through what we hear our friends, our parents, and random people say. I find that in my high school it's because we're all in some way jealous of one another for some weird reason. We ourselves perpetuate the idea of gender roles by criticizing other women for being themselves. Perhaps they dress different, wear shorter dresses, wear lots of makeup, and you catch yourself calling them some very unfavorable words. Calling them loose, or that they make females look bad, that in itself continues the cycle of unnecessary hate toward women who are confident and free. It's important to remember that, yes, we're all struggling to be free and to be ourselves, but that doesn't mean we get to put down others who aren't struggling just because we are or might be jealous. If anything, we should be uplifting those females because they're people to look up to. Being comfortable in yourself is not easy, especially being comfortable in sexuality and body in a world that feeds us nothing but reasons to hate ourselves.

Finding empowerment in other women is so necessary; so is finding empowerment in yourself and it's important to do so. You have to be willing to change, grow, and question your beliefs/what you've been taught. Females empowering other females is so important. To have a safe, welcoming community around you to support you and help you through your lowest and highest points is so important not only because we're social beings and need the connections but because there is no other feeling like having friends that are there for you, to give you compliments, advice, and to answer questions. When I found my group, I began to thrive. I wasn't just living day to day anymore. I finally felt a connection with people who genuinely want/wanted to help me. I stopped wearing baggy XXXL sweaters to school and started dressing up, wearing makeup, and I was doing it for myself. I didn't feel the need to do it because people were telling me I had to. I did it because I wanted to, and the girls just helped me feel comfortable in doing so. I found girls that inspired and continue to inspire me to no end. So many of my unread poems have to deal with them and things we've talked about before just because every time we have a serious conversation together I can't help but to be in awe, and the inspiration just flows out the entire time.

 Although I found my group of people, I personally also know that there aren't many places for teenage girls to connect and form a community. It took me close to nine years to find girls I connected with in that way. If we all recognize that empowerment and inspiration are so important (which they both absolutely are), how come there aren't more all-female safe spaces to make friends, share thoughts, and have meaningful conversations? Why are we scared of creating that community? Truthfully, even I was scared. I was scared of rejection. Deep down we are all scared. We're scared of branching out and having the serious conversations about society and what we're being fed in the media. Social media plays a big part in our lives as well. Deep down I believe that I'm ugly and worthless because that's all I see about fat girls in the mainstream media because our society cares more about looks than positivity or intelligence (which isn't to say that if you are gorgeous you aren't smart; it's just that we never view that side because mainstream media doesn't want us to see it). I don't get to see myself/body type in a positive way. I think other people are also scared of the realization that social media is sometimes very unhealthy. The thing about social media is that, yes, we are surrounded by inspiration and it's amazing to have, but we're also always surrounded by the idea of the "perfect body" and the "perfect woman." Somehow early on we all learn how to repress the feelings that arise from that, but confronting it scares so many of us because we aren't happy with ourselves.

This is why it's so important to find your safe space. To find your space that makes you comfortable, that makes you feel safe. Maybe right now that space is just you by yourself, but don't forget about supporting other women. We're all in this life together; we're all struggling against society and what they want us to be. Find your inspiration in others; find your group. We all need friends that we can trust with our entire hearts. Don't put other women down for being different. Recognize that we're all in different stages of this life. Work on gaining self confidence. If you're brave enough, create a group that's about uplifting others—do art together, share art with each other, talk about the things affecting us all in this society at the moment. Be the change we need. We need more positivity and less competition between us all. No way of being a woman is better than the other. If you like to dress up, dress up. If you like to dress down, dress down. But do it for you. Having a community of support will help you find the confidence to be the very best version of yourself. Try to be the very best version of yourself every day. You never know who you might inspire, who you might help.

MELISSA SMITH

Volunteer at the
Ronald McDonald House,
Changemaker

ABOUT MELISSA SMITH

At the age of fifteen, Melissa was diagnosed with Ewing's Sarcoma, an aggressive form of bone cancer. Over the course of her treatment, she faced many complications but was able to maintain a positive attitude. Now, she gives back to the services that supported her and her family by organizing volunteers at Ronald McDonald Houses.

I like to have control. I like organization. I'm that person who needs to have a hand in everything and know exactly what's happening at all times. I like to know what's expected of me, so I can do my very best. I like to be the best, and I am proud when I am my best. I am an overachiever, and I like to be kept very busy.

I don't like when plans change. Even if the new plan is better, it takes me longer than it probably should to accept it and move on. I pride myself in being honest and empathetic. I enjoy hairstyling and competed in the Skills Alberta Cosmetology section in 2017. I enjoy theater and have been a part of several productions in the community and at school since I was eleven. In my nonexistent spare time, I enjoy crocheting, especially stuffed animals and dolls, and decorating cakes with fondant.

I lived the typical life of a control freak. Now imagine this:

You're sitting at home. Nothing seems out of place or unusual. You have a good routine: wake up, morning religious studies, go to school, go to work, do some homework, an evening extracurricular activity, go to bed, repeat. It's the same story everyday, and you like it. Consistent, plannable, predictable.

Now imagine you're with some friends. You're sitting around, laughing and talking. You lift up your legs and flex your feet—foot. One of them doesn't move. You try again, but no matter how hard you try, you cannot lift up that foot. You remember that in the last few weeks you have tripped more than usual, been a little more clumsy.

Not two weeks later, your knee is unusually sore, and as you pull up your pant leg to investigate, a large lump has manifested, just below the knee on the outside of your right leg. Mom immediately decides to take you into the emergency room the following morning.

Less than forty-eight hours after making that decision, the doctor sits you down and gives you the devastating news. Cancer.

On May 4th, 2017, at the age of fifteen, I was diagnosed with Ewing's Sarcoma, an aggressive form of bone cancer, in my right fibula. In that moment, in that doctor's office, what is now referred to as "the year" in my family began.

I believe I am incredibly lucky. We found my cancer early. A vast majority of bone cancer patients are not diagnosed for months after initial investigation and are in so much pain that they meet their oncologist on a morphine drip. I, on the other hand, was diagnosed less than forty-eight hours after the initial X-ray and did not experience much more than discomfort. Until, that is, the week before I was scheduled to start chemotherapy, when the pain became excruciating. Fortunately, after only one chemotherapy treatment, the pain subsided, and only a few treatments later, the tumor began shrinking noticeably.

Chemotherapy was terrifying. I remember before meeting my oncologist I had absolutely no idea what cancer treatments involved, and I hate the unknown. Within a week or two after that initial appointment, I underwent my first surgery to have an IVAD port placed in my chest. I understood that the port would be a small disc under the skin in my chest that would be accessed with a needle to administer chemo and other IV infusions. I understood the surgery and its purpose—to make chemotherapy and other IV infusions more comfortable—but nothing they told me made me feel any better.

After that initial surgery, and for the next year, my life revolved around my treatments. I alternated between two types of chemo every other week. This meant that each month I spent a minimum of eight nights in the hospital. Every day brought unique challenges, but chemo days were some of the hardest, both physically and emotionally. The day started early with a two-and-a-half-hour drive to the Children's Hospital. I always became overwhelmed by anxiety and negative memories and emotions during that drive. Once we got to the hospital, the fear and anxiety didn't go away.

YOUNG DIVAS THAT CARE

I vividly remember lying in the oncology clinic waiting to be moved to a room. I was trying not to psych myself out before the nurse came in to access my port when a young child on the other side of the curtain let out the most heart-wrenching cry. Of all the emotions I felt in the clinic, the looming fear of the IVAD access and dreading the coming chemo, that child crying was the absolute worst. It was kind of a wake-up call to me. No one should have to go through what I did, but I did. That child did. It is a reality that so many people, young and old, have to face. It sucks, but there is no good reason for me to sit around in self-pity. I have things to do and a life to carry on with, so I need to pick myself up and just do it.

One of the things I had to keep doing was school. I was determined to graduate with my class. I had many people telling me that taking an extra semester isn't a big deal. To me, it is. When I get my mind set on something, I can't let it go. Again, I lucked out, and all of my teachers were understanding and willing to work with me. Although I faced doubt in myself, and from others, I was able to do three core classes and an option class from the hospital. My teachers were able to work closely with me over e-mail so that I could succeed in my classes.

I received so much love and support all through my journey but most especially in the first few weeks. My cosmetology teacher, and more importantly my friend, agreed to cut my hair before I started chemo, so I could have it made into a wig. It was a very emotional day as I said goodbye to fifteen inches of hair. She and a family friend, who is also one of my teachers, organized a hair drive in my honor.

I had a hard time comprehending what was happening to me for a long time, and even still, I sometimes have moments where I think a little too hard and I go back to *What? That happened? That was me?* Everyone talks about how they would handle something like this. I think you don't know. You don't know how you'll react until you need to. And when you need to, you just do. I think the reaction someone has in a time of crisis is very telling of who they are.

The first day of a chemo cycle was really hard. Nothing I did could change the fact that I was filled with lots of negative emotions. It felt like there was always another scary, or painful, or traumatic task ahead of me, no matter what I had just conquered. I've always hated needles, and although I don't scream and cry like I did when I was six, I still hate them. Imagine finding out how many needles you get when you have cancer. During the time that I was home between treatments, I had to learn to give myself a needle. Every day, I needed to inject a medication that would help my blood counts recover faster and allow chemo treatments to happen more frequently. That was very difficult for me, but eventually, I did that too.

I always dreaded getting my IVAD accessed. Because the port lies beneath the skin and feeds into a major vein, to access it requires a one-and-a-half-inch needle to be stabbed into my chest before every cycle, or once a week if I'm admitted longer. My port was especially small and placed in a way that made accessing it difficult and often painful. There were a few specific nurses that could get it on the first try, but it often took two or three tries.

I could always feel the IV fluid going into my body, and the feeling was absolutely sickening. It just felt like a deep cold just seeping into every inch of my body. Sometimes I could smell it or even taste in in my mouth. It was one of those things that I eventually got used to and was absolutely horrified that I'd experienced it enough times to be used to it.

Overall, I tolerated chemotherapy very well, considering the chemicals that are being pumped into my system. Mom and I would hardly ever refer to the chemotherapy as chemo. We called it death juice. When you're in the hospital for that long, you do anything you can to lighten the mood. I always found it comical that the nurses would come in to administer the chemotherapy in big plastic gowns, wearing gloves and a mask, sometimes even goggles, all the while putting the drugs directly into my body.

It took awhile, but my doctor and I found a combination of medications that worked for me. Once we had settled on a series of anti-nausea medications I liked, I didn't suffer from much nausea, just an overall feeling of blah.

That's about where my luck ended. It was only hardships from that point forward. It didn't take long for me to get even more stressed and frustrated than before. I did everything right, but everything went wrong. Nothing I did was good enough, and nobody could tell me why.

In September, I had a tumor resection surgery. It included removing two-thirds of my fibula, partial knee reconstruction, and severing the peroneal nerve. After surgery, my fourteen-inch incision didn't heal. Nobody could tell me why. My team of doctors weren't totally comfortable with the outcome of the surgery. Despite the open wound and the unknown consequences of this plan of action, my doctors decided to add six weeks of radiation therapy to my treatment plan.

During radiation, it still felt like everything was wrong. I suffered severe, debilitating burns from the radiation. I found no effective method of relief until they were so bad that relief was still pain. Even once radiation treatments were over, those burns took excessive amounts of time, even weeks and months, to heal.

Mom and I were able to be home just in time for Christmas. Joke's on me. My blood counts dropped lower than ever on Christmas day. I was at the point where I couldn't walk across the hall from my bedroom to the bathroom without feeling as if I would collapse. To give some perspective, a normal healthy person's hemoglobin sits around one hundred. The hospital will transfuse when someone is at seventy. When I got my blood work, I was at fifty-two. I missed a family gathering to drive to the hospital to get a blood transfusion.

For months, my leg would flare up and seem infected and then settle down and be fine again, over and over. I had it swabbed for infection several times, and never once was there any sign of anything. After Christmas, my surgeon decided to open up my leg to investigate and clean out the dead tissue. What we thought were a couple of spots on my leg that wouldn't close turned out to be almost the entire length just full of necrotic tissue. And yet, there was never an infection. My doctors continued to puzzle over my leg, wondering why it still would not heal.

For the final months of chemo, my doctors tried several methods of wound healing, none of which made any difference. There was a point in time that I routinely had wound debridements and was under an anesthetic twice a week. Still, nothing worked. They hoped now that chemo was over my body would begin to heal on its own, so they sent me home.

It didn't last very long. I had been at school for the first week of the second semester when things went downhill again. My radiation oncologist reached out to my plastic surgeon, who was now in charge of my leg. She suggested that I do hyperbaric oxygen therapy to aid the radiation burns that still hadn't healed and perhaps help the incision. So, I started hyperbaric oxygen therapy. For two and a half hours a day, five days a week, for nearly eight weeks, I laid in a tank of pressurized, 100 percent oxygen. Finally, my leg began to show signs of healing, after six months of being an open wound. A few weeks into the treatment, I got a skin graft to aid healing. By the time all of my treatments were over, and I could finally come home for good, it was one year to the day after I was first diagnosed.

During different portions of my treatment, I was required to be near the hospital for daily appointments but was not admitted. At these times, such as during my radiation treatments and later during hyperbaric oxygen treatments, my mom and I were able to stay at two different Ronald McDonald Houses in Alberta. The time that we spent in these houses was very valuable to me. During this time, we met a woman and her newborn twins, one of whom required extensive medical attention. She became our best friend during that difficult time, and her children became much needed baby therapy for me. Seeing this family brought me so much joy in the midst of the treatments that seemed to have no end.

I will always be thankful for the Ronald McDonald Houses I stayed in. I was always impressed by the extensive facilities and services offered to families almost exclusively from volunteers. It truly was a home away from home.

One of the services offered is called the Home For Dinner program. It involves groups from companies, churches, clubs, etc., coming to the house to cook a homemade meal every day. There was one day in particular that my mom and I were sitting down to eat our dinner and I leaned over to her and commented that I wanted to do this someday, to come and make a meal for the families. I saw myself in the future doing this and loving it. My mom just looked at me and basically said, "Why wait?"

And so, the idea was born. Not long after I was home for good, I reached out and contacted the Ronald McDonald House closest to me and booked four dates. Through everything, my mom kept a Facebook page dedicated to my story, followed by over 500 of my family members, friends, classmates, and community members. I reached out to them for volunteers and donations. I was expecting to need to approach businesses to fundraise the money for the meals, but I was pleasantly surprised to discover just how many people were willing to volunteer their time and donate money. We even got the mayor involved as our master barbecuer! It didn't take long to fill all the volunteer spots and collect enough money to fund those four meals, and more. It really felt like a big community project, and I am just so happy and proud that I was able to make it happen.

Making meals at the Ronald McDonald House helped me develop skills I wouldn't have otherwise. I learned to organize and coordinate groups of people. I learned to meal plan and grocery shop for large groups of people, including potentially picky kids.

Although I can't say I am particularly grateful for cancer, I also can't say I'm not grateful for the things I've learned about myself. While I was on treatment, I really lost touch with who I am. I lost interest in my hobbies. Mom would tell you that I lost many elements of my personality. I just didn't really care about the things that were important to me in "real life." You could say I was broken down to the foundation, to the building blocks of me, and got stuck there for quite some time. As I began to get better, I was able to recognize when little bits of me started coming back. I feel like I have a better understanding of who I really am and who I want to become. It may sound a little backward, but I believe that losing little parts of me and trying to find them again helped me to be more fully me.

If I hadn't gotten cancer, I never would have stayed at the Ronald McDonald House and would have never seen the opportunity to help others.

At my six-month posttreatment checkup, my scans were still clear, with no sign of cancer.

I'm still a control freak. I still like order, but if this journey has taught me anything, it has taught me to be flexible. Not everything in life goes as you plan. Sometimes it's infinitely worse than you planned, and yet, sometimes it is infinitely better.

NATASHA PANDUWAWALA

Founder of
Movement to Remember,
Changemaker

ABOUT NATASHA PANDUWAWALA

Natasha Panduwawala is a graduating high school senior that founded Movement to Remember, an organization dedicated to providing free medical equipment to the disabled Sri Lankan community. Over the course of one year, she raised thousands of dollars and over two hundred orthopedic aids that she delivered to Sri Lankans in need. Today, she works toward nonprofit status and expanding her organization.

My story starts with a 2016 trip to my parents' homeland, Sri Lanka, to attend my cousin's wedding. Although the sole purpose of the trip was to celebrate my cousin and her groom, I asked my mother if we could visit a children's orphanage before we left. Nothing, in particular, spurred me to ask except for sheer curiosity. She happily agreed and arranged for me to visit one that was remote compared to the bustling city of Colombo where we stayed. It took hours but we eventually made it to the orphanage, which happened to be an all-girls orphanage. Upon arrival, the girls greeted us with happy smiles and asked us to take seats. They had prepared a performance for us! For the next hour, each of the girls took turns performing traditional dances, both in groups and as solos. When the last group began the final performance of the evening, the matron leaned over and quietly told me about one of the girls in the group. It was a sweet girl that had the brightest smile who danced as if the music controlled her body. I found out that she had gone through several traumatic experiences as a child that caused some hindrances in her movements and speech. I left the orphanage overwhelmed with emotion. Not only for this girl but for all of the girls in their resilience and undeniable joy. However, there was something about that girl that made me keep on thinking. Her movements, both when she was dancing and not dancing, kept replaying in my mind. When I returned to Colombo, I quickly began to notice the number of Sri Lankans that walked the street with some form of a physical impediment. At every corner, there was someone homeless confined to the curb because they were left with amputated legs. Many elderly people were limping and hunched over as they shopped around marketplaces and grocery stores. I was truly upset by these sights, not only because it was saddening to see how many people were troubled but that I had never noticed this pressing issue before.

As I took my flight home, visions of the girl and these people flashed through my mind. I decided that I could not just return home and pretend to have only seen swaying palm trees and miles of sapphire-blue waters on an island that I call my second home. In reality, I found a population of Sri Lankans that did not have access to medical equipment needed for rehabilitation and recovery. Movement to Remember was my solution to this. My mission was to collect orthopedic aids of every style that could be given to Sri Lankans who truly needed them. I wanted to gather wheelchairs, walkers, canes, boots, crutches, and anything that belonged in a hospital. The search began: I called for my friends to look through their basements for any old equipment they could donate, I called local consignment shops to see if they had items they could sell to me for cheap prices, and I posted across Facebook to connect with people who could also help. I accumulated masses of walkers and wheelchairs and crutches in my basement. With the help of my younger brother, we spent every Sunday morning organizing and cataloging each item.

About halfway through the collection process, I realized that there were families that benefited from donating their old orthopedic aids. For these families, this donation was a healing experience to be letting go of equipment that belonged to their deceased loved ones. I quickly learned that my organization not only benefited disabled Sri Lankans but also individuals and families trying to gain closure. My job was simply to connect the two worlds so that they could help one another.

After nine months, I collected over 200 orthopedic aids, valued at over $13,000. I was ecstatic that I reached my goal of 200 donations, but I soon faced a new problem: how was I to get all of these items overseas? With the help of my dad, I found a Sri Lankan shipping company that carries bulk goods directly to Sri Lanka. They agreed to come to my home, where I stored all of the items, and take them to their shipping dock. Furthermore, since the shipment was for a good cause, they agreed to discount the costs! The cost of the shipment was based on how much space my items would take in the container, but since we had not packed anything yet, I could not come up with an estimate. I spent the last couple of months raising as much money as I could, hoping that it would be enough to cover the expenses. I looked to the Sri Lankan communities in Maryland and DC to help me. Each of them rallied together and pooled more than $4,000 to pay for shipping expenses and import taxes. The day the shipping company came to my house, it was such a relief to know that everything was covered. A team of my dad's friends came over to dismantle every item and press them to each other on wooden palettes. This process took more than five hours between the seven of us. Not only did we have to dismantle and pack each item, but we had to catalog everything again and haul it up the stairs from the basement. We finished right as the shipping truck backed into my driveway.

After packing day, the momentum continued into June of 2017 where I dedicated the month to traveling across Southwest Sri Lanka to hand-deliver each donation to its recipient. I made a promise to each donor that I would personally see who their donation was affecting. No matter how far a single walker was going, I would be sure to accompany it on its journey. At the beginning of the month, I targeted several elderly orphanages. I was astounded to see the number of elders that stayed in bed all day simply because they did not have the equipment they needed to move about. Afterward, I distributed to the homeless and a few hospitals. One hospital was so excited for all of the walkers and wheelchairs to come that they hosted a celebration where Buddhist monks were invited to bless the patients and their new aid. I was thrilled to be included in these celebrations and learn more about the divine culture of my Sri Lanka.

Of all of the donations, a wheelchair given to a girl named Randika was my favorite, by far. Randika was about six years old and suffered from cerebral palsy. Her family did not have the means to buy a wheelchair for her, let alone one of the wheelchairs designed specifically for those with cerebral palsy. Even in America, they are expensive and are costly when it comes to customization. Luckily, one family had donated a wheelchair that belonged to their son that had cerebral palsy. In fact, he was about six years old when he had that chair. Before even arriving in Sri Lanka, I sought help from my family that lived there to find someone that could have this wheelchair. Finding someone that perfectly fit into that chair was no easy feat given that the chair was customized and fitted. They found Randika as a match, and when I brought the wheelchair to her home, she was indeed a perfect match. For Randika's family, it became easy to strap her into the wheelchair to take her shopping. Before, Randika did not have the opportunity to go out much or experience the outdoors. She spent a lot of time lying on the floor of her living room with her favorite toys (Randika could not sit up for too long to stay in a chair). Yet, her new wheelchair allowed her to sit with her family, travel with her family, and play with her family. Stories like Randika's were not uncommon for many of the other recipients. For far too long, they could not access proper medical equipment so they could live a normal life.

At the conclusion of my month in Sri Lanka, I took a flight back to my small town. I brainstormed ways that I could expand Movement to Remember, ways that I could keep such a project going. I decided that I was going to make Movement to Remember a nonprofit organization. In obtaining this status, I could continue in my endeavors to provide medical equipment as a trusted organization.

Today, I have plenty of wheelchairs and walkers in my basement that are awaiting their turn to arrive in Sri Lanka. Families are still donating to my cause! Someone even dug through their attic and found boxes of brand-new teaching supplies and textbooks for grade school. Not only will I be distributing orthopedic aids, but I will be finding schools to give these books to as well. I do not want to limit the number of Sri Lankans that can be helped under any circumstances.

YOUNG DIVAS THAT CARE

Through the entire process of raising Movement to Remember and successfully completing my first project, I learned that no one is ever too young, too old, or too inexperienced to make an impact on our world. Too many times I have heard people being discouraged from taking action because their "time is up" or they "do not think they are capable" of leading forth such an effort. But at fifteen years old I helped more than 200 people with little experience in organizing large projects. Take a chance on yourself. Give yourself the chance to show what it is you're capable of doing in this world.

I am thrilled and excited for my next shipment to Sri Lanka. As soon as I receive nonprofit status for Movement to Remember, I am set to take the next flight over!

MEGAN LOH
Founder of
GEARup4Youth &
STEMup4Youth

ABOUT MEGAN LOH

Through her passion, Megan Loh, founder and president of GEARup4Youth, has been bridging the gender gap and empowering girls around the world to pursue science and technology since 2015. She has received national recognition in the President's Gold Volunteer Service Award, Prudential Spirit of Community Award, Girl Scouts Gold Award, Aspirations in Computing and more, and has spoken on an international platform at the United Nations Headquarters.

A little bulldozer barreled toward me at full speed as I was staggering out the door of the Boys and Girls Club with boxes of LEGO robots stacked in my arms. Her velocity almost knocked the robots out of my hands! Clinging onto my leg like a koala, she pleaded, "Can I pleeease keep my robot a little longer? I just figured out how to make it move in a circle! I reaaallly like robotics! I want to build big robots when I grow up!" She released my leg temporarily to stretch out her arms as wide as she could. "This big!"

It was little Melissa. Like most of the other girls I teach in my weekly robotics classes at the Boys and Girls Club, Melissa rides the bus to the club after school each day, because her parents are too busy working to support their family to watch over her after school.

She was the girl who turned away when I first introduced robotics to my class. I still vividly remember what she told me that day.

As the other girls scattered to work on their robots, I pulled her aside and asked, "What's wrong? Why don't you want to build these fun LEGO robots?"

"Dad said robotics is for boys. Girls don't learn programming."

Her words struck me. When I was around her age, I was fortunate enough to attend a few technology-related summer camps. I was shocked at the first camp I went to—it was the first time I had ever seen the boys' restroom line almost ten times longer than the girls' line before! There were twenty boys in my class and only one other girl besides me. That was when I first saw how large the gender gap in the technology industry truly is. Subsequent camps only confirmed my realization. Since then, I've constantly noticed how girls are hindered by the influence of gender stereotypes.

As Melissa was pouting in front of me, I wondered, *How many more girls are out there who don't want to pursue technology just because they were told they couldn't?*

"Melissa, do you like flowers?" I asked.

"Yeah! Flowers are my favorite!"

"Look at this flower I built out of LEGOs! Isn't it cool?"

"Wow! That's so cute! I want one!"

I smiled at her as she grabbed the flower from my hands and inspected it. "You can build it yourself! Let me show you how."

I showed her the first piece, and she happily grabbed the next piece, clicking them into place. Time flew by as we worked together to design the flower.

"Look, Miss Megan! Look what I've made!" She grabbed my hand excitedly, embracing her new creation in her other hand. "Can I make it move? How does it work?"

I was elated to see her taking the initiative to learn how to program her creation. We made our way over to a laptop.

"All we have to do is use the mouse to drag these code blocks and line them up together. Now let's press the green button and see what happens!"

"I love it! This is so cool!" Melissa exclaimed, tapping the green button over and over again. "Look, Miss Megan, it's moving!"

"Do you think it was hard to program your robot?"

"Not at all! I want to do more! Wow, look at this one! I want to build a helicopter next!"

After the progression she had made from reluctance to exuberance, there was no way I could say no to her request. I smiled down at her little puppy face and relented. "Yes, of course!"

There is nothing more amazing than making a difference in a girl's life. A simple act such as sharing what I am passionate about can make so much of a difference for the girls around me.

The gratitude of young girls like Melissa truly showed me how priceless teaching is. The joy of helping others is such an indescribable feeling!

Every Friday as my volunteers and I walk toward the Boys and Girls Club, my eyes immediately catch Melissa's face peeking out from behind the door, waiting for us to bring another day of joy and robotics. As soon as she spots our bright blue shirts, she dashes out of the doorway and flings her arms around my waist in a mini bear hug.

YOUNG DIVAS THAT CARE

"Miss Megan, Miss Megan, what are we going to build today?" she inquires, her eyes full of curiosity.

Technology is the future of our modern world. Women only hold 10–20 percent of tech-related jobs, while minorities and the underprivileged only account for 5 percent. I founded the nonprofit organization GEARup4Youth in 2015. With the help of over 130 volunteers from twenty-five different schools, I've been able to affect over 6,500 girls by fostering their interests in technology through weekly classes, presentations, and the book that I authored. It's so wonderful to see girls like Melissa grow from rejecting technology to never wanting to stop building, learning, and creating!

MAHEALANI SIMS-TULBA
Founder of
B.R.A.V.E. Hawaii,
Miss Teen Cosmos
United States 2019

ABOUT
MAHEALANI SIMS-TULBA

Mahealani Sims-Tulba is eighteen years old and a graduate of Sacred Hearts Academy in Honolulu, Hawaii. She is currently a freshman at the University of Hawaii. She loves to sing Broadway music and is very active in musical theater.

She was chosen as Hawaii's Top High School Finalist for the 2018 Prudential Spirit of Community Award, and she also received the 2018 Violet Richardson Soroptomist of Waikiki Award, the 2018 Western Regional Violet Richardson Soroptomist Award, and has earned five Gold Level Presidential Volunteer Service Awards. She is currently planning the launch of her new TV show, *B.R.A.V.E. HAWAII TV*.

Ever since I was a little girl, I knew that I wanted to help people. I have always wanted to make people smile or make them feel a little better about themselves. When I was in the fifth grade, I entered my first pageant. At first, I loved what I was doing; I was able to make others feel good through community service, while also learning to be more confident and how to make myself a better person. I was having so much fun giving back to the community, I wanted to get all my friends involved.

One day at school, I had decided to tell my best friends about how I entered a pageant, and I wanted all of them to be there to support me. I expected my friends to be so excited for me. However, I was ridiculed and shamed.

You're not smart enough to be in pageants. You're not pretty enough to be in pageants. You're too fat to be in pageants.

These words really hurt me. At ten years old, this is when I was starting to finally find myself and learn what I wanted to do. Even though my friends said these words about me, I tried to stay strong. I tried to not let the mean and nasty words get to me, and I still competed in the pageant.

The following year, I had entered another pageant and I had won. I was so excited because I had worked so hard for something that I had really wanted. I was so proud of myself and I knew that it was something that I wanted to continue doing.

Somehow, the word that I won the pageant had gotten to my school. The following Monday, it was announced during our school assembly that I had won. There were people who congratulated me, but rumors about me began to spread. Someone had said that I did not really win the pageant but that I was just given the title because the judges of the pageant felt bad for me. I was devastated. I had worked so hard to prove myself, and within minutes it was ruined by a couple of rumors.

I tried to not let any of the words get to me. I tried to stay strong and continue living the best way that I could. But after a while, the weight of the rumors and bullying over the course of several years got so bad I broke down.

Luckily, I had a very supportive family and they helped me out of the horrible situation I was in. It was something that I never wanted to be in again, and I was sure that there were other kids just like me who went through the same things as me—maybe even worse. That's when I knew that I wanted to do something.

I wanted to be able to tell my story in a fun and exciting way but also be able to spread a positive message that would stick with kids. That is when I decided to write a book called *It's Okay To Be Different*. It was something that I worked so hard on, and I was fortunate enough to go to different schools and libraries in Hawaii and share my story though my book. After a while, I knew that I wanted to do more. I wanted to be able to reach others and help as many people as I could. That's when I thought of B.R.A.V.E. Hawaii. I knew that with a foundation I would be able to extend my reach further than school libraries.

I started B.R.A.V.E. Hawaii—a nonprofit, anti-bullying foundation—in 2013 when I was thirteen years old. B.R.A.V.E. is an acronym and it stands for "Be Respectful and Value Everyone." We not only teach about the bullying problem, but we also talk about setting achievable goals and making the right choices. We also teach about the dangers of drug and alcohol abuse, as well as the importance of taking care of yourself and your environment.

I have been so blessed with B.R.A.V.E. Hawaii. Not only has it changed the lives of so many people here in the state of Hawaii, but it has also changed my life. I always thought that I would live with my bullying experience and let it impact my life negatively. But I did not want to do that—I wanted to make a change. I wanted to take the dark time in my life and bring light to others. I wanted to let people know that I was there for them. B.R.A.V.E. Hawaii has given me the opportunity to touch the lives of many people. My bullying story is something that I would never want anyone to go through, but I don't wish that it did not happen to me. Without it, I would not have been able to create B.R.A.V.E. Hawaii and make a difference in the world.

RILEY CALLEN
Youth Philanthropist,
Founder of Be Brave for Life

ABOUT RILEY CALLEN

Riley Callen is a sophomore at Burr and Burton Academy in Manchester, VT. Riley founded Be Brave for Life, a nonprofit that raises money and awareness for benign brain tumors, in 2015 after she got her second benign brain tumor removed. Riley plays field hockey, lacrosse, and in the winter, she teaches snowboarding.

My name is Riley Callen and I am a sixteen-year-old sophomore at Burr and Burton Academy in Manchester, Vermont. When I was eight years old, I think it is safe to say that my life changed. I was diagnosed with my first benign brain tumor, which began the journey that made me who I am today. See, I started experiencing symptoms, such as slight facial palsy on the left side of my face. After several doctor's visits and MRIs, doctors discovered a benign brain tumor in my brain stem. Being benign (noncancerous) made it less daunting to treat, but by the tumor being in the brain stem—the part of the brain that controls all the basic functions—it was just as life-threatening. I have always been very optimistic, so due to not really knowing the magnitude of the situation and my optimism, I wasn't very frightened by the idea of a craniotomy. The corrective surgical procedure would include the removal of part of the bone from my skull to expose my brain.

Additionally, out of my siblings, I was always the one who went with the flow. I knew that no matter what happened, it would all end up being OK. My confidence definitely helped me during the following years. My first surgery was unsuccessful and definitely the hardest. My surgeon in New York declared my tumor as inoperable after more than six hours of surgery. It required the longest recovery period and I don't remember much of it at all, except that I was confused, nervous, and tingly all over. I remember feeling hurt that I had to go through all of it for nothing. I also vividly remember declining ice cream, as I was miserable and had no appetite. The failed craniotomy and long recovery process made me realize for the first time what I was up against. I knew then that it wasn't going to be the walk-in-the-park experience that I had hoped it would be.

A few weeks after surgery, as soon as I started to feel like myself again, it was safe to fly to Arizona to Dr. Spetzler. We hoped to be able to remove my previously named "inoperable" tumor. Dr. Spetzler successfully removed my brain tumor on October 3rd, 2011 and we were over the moon about it. Afterward, the follow-up visits and procedures were all a blur. I was constantly in and out of hospitals. I had a total of four surgeries. One was to install my Bone Anchored Hearing Aid (BAHA) implant to improve my hearing. I also had two reconstructive facial surgeries so I could smile. Another surgery was to insert a small weight on my eyelid so I could close my eye.

In June of 2014, my family and I moved to Pawlet, Vermont from Chatham, New Jersey. After living there for seven months, my parents sat me down and told me that my annual MRI had shown another tumor in the same spot as the previous one. Whether it had regrown or the doctor didn't get all of it the last time, they didn't know. It didn't matter to me. I was mad. I didn't show it, but I was mad at the world and kept wondering why this had to happen to me. That said, I was grateful that it was me and not someone else. I had dealt with it once and I had very little doubt that I could do it all over again. My parents and I returned to Arizona that January with the single perk of being able to go to my favorite restaurant—a twelve-year-old's dream—an all-you-can-eat steakhouse.

The surgery went smoothly and I was back to my regular self in record time. Regardless, I was bothered by the fact that kids—my age, younger, and older—were or would have to go through the same thing that I did. I wouldn't change anything in my life. Sure, I've gone through things and struggled, but the lessons I've learned and the greater appreciation I have every day has helped with making peace with that. What I realized, though, is that there are kids who don't make it. Some of the kids that do survive the surgery may have bigger consequences to major brain surgery. Their complications may be more serious than losing their hearing in one ear and looking different on one side of their face.

In 2015, I started an organization called "Be Brave for Life." My mom and I hosted a hike-a-thon and a basket bonanza and have successfully operated it for four years now. Our mission is to show people that benign tumors aren't always harmless. We raise money to find an alternative treatment that doesn't involve brain surgery. Over the past four years, through Be Brave for Life, we have raised $550,000 in charitable donations. Running this organization has taught me a lot and I am so grateful for that. I'm not mad anymore about what I had to go through. If anything, I am happy with what my mom and I were able to accomplish because of it.

DANIKA GORDON
Author, Supporter of
Books 4 Kids

ABOUT DANIKA GORDON

After an experience with being bullied in second grade, Danika Gordon from South Dakota wanted to do more to help prevent bullying by encouraging kindness. At age twelve, she wrote and illustrated an online storybook titled *What Makes You a Superhero?* She has since authored two additional books, offering positive and inspirational messages to youth.

"You are stupid," my classmate hissed at me. I remember the first time she said it to me. At first, I was taken aback and thought, *Why is she saying that to me?* But the hateful comments continued over several weeks whenever our teacher was out of sight. I was called stupid, ugly, and other hurtful names over and over again by this same student; occasionally others chimed in. I found myself scared, angry, sad. My heart ached; my confidence faltered; I no longer enjoyed school. And I often wondered, *What had I done to make this other student dislike me so much?*

That was second grade. I eventually got the courage to tell my mom about my experiences at school, and she immediately initiated a meeting with the school counselor and my classroom teacher. After they were made aware of the situation, the other student was reprimanded, and I was fortunate that the bullying stopped. It took some time, but eventually with support from my family and teachers, my enjoyment of school returned and I found a circle of friends who helped my confidence—and my smile—return. But while things went back to "normal" for me, the mark from bullying was left on my heart.

Over the next few years in elementary school, I watched as other students were bullied. Name calling, forceful pushing and shoving, shunning, or embarrassing comments. I never had to look too far to see someone being targeted like I had been. I knew their pain, and I would try to help by asking others to stop their rude behavior, but it was typically ignored. It felt like one small voice couldn't make a difference.

Throughout these years, I was also involved in the youth development program called 4-H. I had the opportunity to meet other youth who were focused on leadership, citizenship, and community service. I experienced firsthand how rewarding it was to work on projects together, set a positive example, and donate my time to service efforts from working at the local food pantry to gathering books to donate to children in need to picking up litter at the city park. Most importantly, I learned about character traits of a good citizen, including respect, responsibility, fairness, caring, and being trustworthy. My experiences in 4-H helped fill my heart with excitement, joy, and love. I began to think, *This must be what it feels like to be a superhero!*

And then the idea came to me: each of us has the ability to be kind—and that is what can make us our very own superhero!

Rather than telling others to stop bullying, I wanted to focus my efforts on encouraging kids to be kind and change the world with one kind action at a time. I decided a children's storybook would be a great way to share that message with a large audience. I knew both a teacher and a family friend who had written their own children's books, and my mom is a freelance writer for agricultural publications, so I had seen other people write throughout my upbringing and just believed I could be a writer too.

I found an online public website (Storyjumper.com) that allowed me to create and illustrate my story on their website for no charge. The book could then be viewed for free online and soft and hardcover books could be purchased. So I dove into the project. I created my book titled *What Makes You A Superhero?* I kept the book simple so that elementary students would grasp the message that each of us has the amazing ability to be kind. I also included a "discussion questions section" at the back of my book so it would prompt self-reflection among readers and help reinforce the book's positive message of spreading kindness. At the time, I was twelve years old and in sixth grade.

My family ordered a few keepsake hardcover copies, and word began to spread that I had written a book. I was invited to local elementary classrooms and library story hours to share my book with others. Soon my story was featured in the newspaper and even more people wanted to know about my book. I was delighted that more and more people were learning about my message of kindness. Meanwhile, through the StoryJumper website, teachers and students were also finding my book online. One day I received a message from a teacher in New Zealand saying she enjoyed sharing my book with her classroom. I was amazed! It felt wonderful to know that the message of kindness was being shared, and hopefully, helping to make our world a better place. (To date, more than 60,000 readers have viewed my book on the StoryJumper website.)

After a few years, as an eighth grader, I had an idea to write a second book. Working with a retired teacher who had become my mentor, we researched historical people from my home state of South Dakota and created a storyline that encourages kids to dream big, just like their South Dakotan ancestors. We self-published this book, and I have shared it with many South Dakotan classrooms.

At about the same time, I was contacted by a South Dakota-based publisher who had established the Books 4 Kids program, which publishes books with support from local sponsors and then conducts author visits to elementary classrooms and donates a book to each child. The Books 4 Kids program is focused on sharing books that help kids learn about good character traits. The publisher invited me to create a book building off my inaugural superhero storybook, and so I authored my third book titled *Superhero Surprise*. Over the last three years, I have done several classroom visits, as well as virtual visits with classrooms via Skype or FaceTime. It's a great opportunity to surprise kids with the message that they can each be a superhero by being kind. I also have an opportunity to tell them about my own experiences of overcoming bullying—and I always encourage them to dream big and maybe they will become an author one day too. Through the Books 4 Kids program several thousand of my books have been donated to elementary children across the United States.

As I reflect on all of these experiences, I am in awe. I was able to take a difficult experience from second grade, and through the love and support of my family, teachers, friends, and fellow 4-H youth, I have had an amazing journey of spreading a positive message about kindness. I have received several awards and recognition along the way, including being recognized by South Dakota First Lady Linda Daugaard and earning the Prudential Spirit of Community award in 2016. But most important to me has been sharing the message that kindness can make a difference, and each and every one of us have the ability to be kind. I hope that everyone will remember that one small act of kindness is like tossing a stone into the water—it creates a ripple effect that circles out and impacts everything around us.

MADELENE KLEINHANS
Founder of
Heartfelt Hugs

ABOUT
MADELENE KLEINHANS

Madelene is a junior at Colorado Virtual Academy where she is the Honor Society President. She also plays softball and does theater with the local high school. She started Heartfelt Hugs by Madelene Cares nonprofit when she was twelve and her brother was in treatment for cancer.

When I was eight years old, my brother was diagnosed with acute lymphoblastic leukemia. He was five at the time, and I remember the day that my parents found out they rushed him to the hospital and I was dropped off at one of my mom's friend's house. I was too young to fully understand what was going on with my brother and why my family was never home. As time progressed, my brother got further in his treatment, and I started to understand a little bit more. I felt very abandoned because I was never seeing any of my family because they were in the hospital with my brother all the time and whenever anyone would stop by they would be greatly concerned with my brother and it was almost like I didn't exist. Over the years of my brother's treatment, I started to become more and more aggressive and angry. As a very troubled kid, I got in a lot of trouble wherever I went and I even managed to get kicked out of a summer camp. I was trying to get attention by using negative energy and actions. No one fully understood what I felt because I would not open up to people, so I was just constantly getting yelled at and it felt like the whole world was against me.

My parents enrolled me in counseling and I started going to support groups for siblings and families of kids who are critically ill. After meeting kids my age who were also in the same position, I started to realize that I was not alone and finally started to understand what was going on and that my brother was going to be OK. So after talking to many counselors at the Children's Hospital and other families, I got more hope and I began to realize I could make something good out of the situation.

One day when we went in for my brother's chemo therapy appointment, I learned that there was a little chest full of toys that all of the cancer kids and critically ill children were allowed to pick a toy out of after they finished their treatment. I was very bored since I'd been sitting in the hospital for a couple of hours waiting for my brother to get his treatment, and I politely asked the nurses if I could pick something out of the chest. They immediately said no and explained how the toys were only meant for the kids who were critically ill. That kind of frustrated me, so after thinking about it for a while, I came up with the idea that I wanted a toy chest for the siblings. I started presenting my idea to people and I talked to some of the coordinators at the Children's Hospital. I started presenting my idea at events and fundraisers, and people began to donate money and choice toys to go into the chest. We even had someone who volunteered to paint a mural on the toy chest! Soon it really started to work, and the people in the Children's Hospital were helping me get the idea on its feet. Before too long, I had hundreds of toys and a ton of donations for the toy chest, but after the process went on for a long time, it started to feel like it was never ending and the toy chest was never going to work. So after about two years of trying to get the toy chest into the Children's Hospital, I came to realization that there was just too much red tape and my idea wasn't going to work. So now I was stuck with a ton of toys and donations that people intended to go toward this idea, and I realized I couldn't just let all of that go to waste. One day I was sitting with my mom and she had the idea to create a support group for the siblings of kids with critical illnesses. So there was this organization called There With Care (a nonprofit that helps families of critically ill kids) that was donating food to our family, and we started talking to them about a support group and wondering if they would want to pair up with us.

There With Care was thrilled to want to help us make the support group come true so we had several meetings over several months. The original idea was that we were going to have a therapist come in and talk to the kids and then we were going to do fun things and hand out the toys to the kids and their families. In one of the meetings we were talking to the therapist and I realized that I didn't want the kids to have to talk about any of the problems going on at home. I wanted my support group to be a time for them to be free and not have to worry about any of their problems. So right then and there I told the therapist that we really appreciated her time but we would not be needing her help. Everyone was confused with my decision, but I explained it and then everyone supported me. That's when Heartfelt Hugs by Madelene Cares really started to form. Our first event consisted of only three people, two other siblings and me. The next meeting had about ten people, and then after that, the meetings began to double and triple in attendance. Now we sometimes have over one hundred people attending our regular event.

When families come to me, crying at events, thanking me for starting Heartfelt Hugs by Madelene Cares, and saying that their child needed this program so much, I feel so thankful to everyone who has helped make this program so successful. There is no age limit for finding a solution to a problem. I was only twelve when I started Heartfelt Hugs by Madelene Cares, but I listened to my mom who said, "Stop complaining about the problem and figure out a solution!" And I did!

Amber Nelson
Founder of
Amber's Animal Outreach,
Animal Activist

ABOUT
AMBER NELSON

Amber S. Nelson founded Amber's Animal Outreach, a Florida 501c3, at just thirteen years old, in 2014. AAO's focus is on abused, neglected, and at-risk dogs in high-kill shelters. Amber is an advocate for kindness, education, and the importance of spaying/neutering. Like most teens, she enjoys shopping and spending time with friends and family along with baking, crafting, and country music. She is originally from and resides in Palm Beach County, Florida.

I have always been very shy and quiet. Talking to people I didn't know well was extremely uncomfortable. However, the one thing I could easily talk about to anyone is animals. Ever since I was very young, I have loved animals, especially dogs. My parents would take me on golf cart rides around the neighborhood just so I could give treats to the dogs (permission granted from owners). Dogs are always so accepting and sweet.

Even after the worst day, when I come home from school, my dogs are so happy to see me. I forget about all the events of the day and worries and surround myself with my dogs' happy attitudes. They immediately put a smile on my face.

With my mom, Kelly, I have volunteered with many dog rescues since I was seven years old. Years later, I realized some dogs were no longer in the shelter but had not been adopted. I learned they had been euthanized, due to shelter capacity constraints, or needed medical attention (which there were no funds). Rescue groups were full or did not have the space or extra money to give these poor souls the chance they deserved. I felt so bad. Those terrible feelings of sadness and helplessness haunted me. I was only a kid, not even a bona fide rescuer or a nonprofit organization.

I wanted to do more than just give treats and belly rubs. My dream was to work toward saving and helping dogs, especially those who had been neglected, abused, and/or abandoned. I could never imagine how anyone would want to hurt a poor, innocent animal. Dogs are so loyal, sharing unconditional love.

I knew I had to do something that your typical teenager doesn't. I asked my parents if I could start my own nonprofit dog rescue so I had a say in helping dogs in need. Yes, I may be shy, but when there are dogs that need help, look out because I suddenly go into overdrive! It doesn't matter if they have behavioral or health issues. I weed the ones out who I know we can help.

Amber's Animal Outreach was granted official status as a Florida 501c3 in July 2014. Even though I was just thirteen years old, this was a major accomplishment. I felt on top of the world! To date we have rescued, vetted, fostered, and rehomed hundreds of dogs.

There is no stopping me. Juggling school, friends, and the normal things teenagers are into—I went into action. I was able to obtain death row dogs, scheduled for euthanization due to space constraints at high kill shelters. Innocent animals that had been burned, shot, neglected, abused, and even those that were heartworm positive could now have a chance at a happy life. Helping those dogs get medical attention, rehabbed, and find them their forever loving families fills my heart with joy. I beam when I hear of our dogs enjoying life and being spoiled.

One special case was a young redbone hound mix. He came into Amber's Animal Outreach in December 2015. Emaciated, he weighed only thirty-two pounds and was estimated to be under two years old. We named him Quin, vetted him, got him healthy, good house manners, and found him a wonderful family. He is the only pet in the household and the "apple of his mom's eye!" He enjoys running in the dog park, long walks, and massage and acupuncture treatments. Now eighty pounds, he is happy, healthy, and living a wonderful life!

Every year on March 3 my birthday, Amber's Animal Outreach alumni and families are invited to lunch and a reunion. It makes my heart sing with joy to see how well the dogs are all doing, now being a part of loving families.

Over the past four years, I have learned more than I could have ever imagined, ranging from medical treatments, alternatives, the importance of vaccines, spaying/neutering, and especially training. Many pets end up homeless because people don't take the time or energy to properly socialize and/or train their pet. Just like children, pets need a strong leader, loving guidance, and boundaries.

I am learning valuable skills to take into adulthood, organizing weekly adoption events at local pet supply stores, golf tournaments, fundraisers, and an array of holiday events. Especially popular is our special Puppy Bowl fundraiser—puppies playing football, even scoring touchdowns! I am learning and honing valuable interpersonal skills by arranging vendors, food, music, face painting, sponsors, and finding volunteers to handle dogs and help set up at the event. This is all so worth it. We raise awareness and funds for the dogs we assist and fund medical expenses and care of these beautiful, loving creatures, while they await their "furever homes."

I will continue to rescue, rehab, and rehome dogs. We enjoy finding loving homes for as many dogs as we are capable (space, energy, and monetarily) of helping. I realize I cannot save the world but I sure can make a difference—one dog at a time.

Those terrible feelings of sadness or hopelessness are gone. I am beyond grateful for all I have learned, whom I have met, and how this has all changed my life, for the better. Even though I still consider myself an introvert, I cannot deny that my confidence and communication skills have improved, tremendously. I go out and educate the community about the welfare of animals. It makes me feel very complete having made a difference in so many (two- and four-legged) lives. Experiencing how I can influence the community (youth to adults) to help dogs, and educate them on animal welfare is very rewarding. I highly recommend you to think big and follow your passion. You will find success.

Lucille Johnstone
Poet and Activist

ABOUT
LUCILLE JOHNSTONE

Lucille is a teenager living in Abbotsford, BC with her mother and two brothers. She experienced a traumatic situation when she lost her Uncle Curtis who overdosed in 2017. Curtis was her best friend. She enjoys hanging out with friends, listening to music, and doing hair and makeup.

GONE

My tragedy struck me like a lightning bolt
He was gone and he wasn't coming back.
I was informed of his death a week after it happened.
It seemed as if everyone knew except me.
He was different, you see.
I had always thought about what I'd say,
not knowing that he would die that day.
Not knowing that it was your last, I said I hate you
and I scream in your face, I only said that because
I thought I'd see you soon.
But no, I felt like I was stuck in a helium balloon
going up and up getting farther from the ground
He didn't die because of a stab, shot, or a drown
No, it was an overdose
A drug overdose
He once said don't do drugs they're gross
He did
And he died
A beautiful person, now so cold
Of an uncle whose life was basically sold
There is a missing piece in my heart
that no one could fill
There's one thing you should know,
I miss you, uncle, and I always will.
He once said that he will never leave
And that lie stuck me
And I still sit here and grieve.

Meagan Warren
Founder of Books For Bedtime,
active member in Mensa

ABOUT MEAGAN WARREN

Meagan Warren is a sixteen-year-old changemaker who is passionate about words. She runs her own nonprofit, Books for Bedtime, and is an Ashoka Young Changemaker and a member of Mensa. Diagnosed with the chronic disease POTS, which makes her life more challenging, she is a fighter who wants nothing more than to make the world a better place!

Books have always been in my life; even when I was little, my mom would read to me. It is because of this that I learned to read at the age of two and, later on, founded Books For Bedtime. Ever since that fateful day, when I first discovered my love, my passion, my fuel, I have always had a book with me. So of course, having always had books around me, finding out that there were children my age who didn't have books at their beck and call was unimaginable at first. My mom has taught in urban book deserts my whole life. I remember very clearly my first experience realizing just how close to home book deserts were. I was visiting my mom at her school on my day off when we all went down to her school library. I remember heading over to browse the shelves to see what interesting books there might be and then being horrified when I realized how few books there were on the shelves. There were only three shelves full of books. Three. That means that there wasn't even a full shelf of books for each grade in her K-6 school. I had known that book deserts existed, but I did not realize just how close to home they were.

As I grew older, the problem became more and more apparent to me. I both witnessed and read about book deserts. In a book desert, there is only one book for every 300 children who live in the poorest areas of the United States. I would come to find that my mom's school was not alone. Columbus has several areas that are book deserts. Eventually I decided that something had to be done about this crisis. It is because of this realization that I founded Books For Bedtime and, in doing so, found my power.

When I first started Books For Bedtime I only planned on donating at schools; since then I have donated at schools, homeless shelters, food pantries, new immigrant organizations, and a local furniture bank, as well as to school and classroom libraries. My goal when I started Books For Bedtime was to assist 500 children the first year by donating books to them through low-income schools. I not only met this goal but exceeded it by over 5,500 books that first year. As of April 2019, I have donated over 86,000 books to children in need, with most being distributed in Central Ohio, along with the Cincinnati, Dayton, and Cleveland areas. My books have even traveled to Texas, to help restock school libraries ravished by hurricanes. I don't think that I would have reached my goal if my story had not been first published in *This Week Bexley*, a local newspaper.

As soon as I was featured in the newspaper, book donations started flying in. I would walk home from school to randomly find boxes of books on my front stoop. In addition to donating books to children, I have also encouraged children to read more and to start making an impact like I have with Books For Bedtime. I had no idea that kids would be inspired by my speeches, but they have been! I absolutely love that my impact in making a difference is growing! I have had parents e-mail me and tell me that their children want to hold book drives and help with sorting and stamping books as well. One time, a six-year-old in my community collected books, with the help of her mom. I love that she is so young and has already decided that she can make a difference in the world, and I am so proud that my activity with Books For Bedtime has helped!

In December 2016, I spoke to 500 middle school students in nearby Grove City, Ohio. The students were lucky, in that a majority of them could afford books without the assistance of Books For Bedtime. Instead, I was asked to speak to them as they began their unit on activism. It was a wonderful experience. I then sat with a teacher-selected panel of ten students, and they were able to ask me specific questions about Books For Bedtime. They took my information and ideas and replicated them so that they could help other charities as well. They also held a book drive for me and collected over 4,000 books!

Seeing their enthusiasm for change and their desire to help others inspired me to start another initiative, the Changemaker Folder. I saw their passion for change, a passion that very much mirrored my own, and felt this strong desire to help them on their changemaking journey. I knew that I couldn't personally mentor every student, so I came up with the Changemaker Folder. The folders are meant to serve as a resource, a guide, and an inspiration. I want to make sure that every youth realizes their power to change the world. I had no idea just how powerful a story could be, when I first started Books For Bedtime.

When I first started Books For Bedtime, I only had a State of Ohio nonprofit license. Once Books For Bedtime became more well-known, and grew so much, I applied for and received my 501(c)(3) public charity license. That allowed me to receive financial donations so that I could begin to travel more easily outside of Central Ohio. It also allowed me to post on Volunteermatch.org. Through that website, I was able to find a website designer that created a website for me for free! Having a 501(c)(3) 5license has allowed adults, I think, to take my passion much more seriously.

Starting Books For Bedtime has taught me so much! One of the things that I've learned about myself is that I am a good public speaker. I had given speeches before I started Books For Bedtime, but those were presentations that I had, for the most part, planned out quite well in advance. With the speeches I give for Books For Bedtime, I have created index cards with bullet points on them. However, I don't use them most times; they are there just in case I forget a key talking point. I also take questions from the students after I finish my speech. I have learned to think very quickly on my feet!

I now partner regularly with groups of people who want to help out the community. I host "stamping and sorting" parties in my home. I have six to eight people come to my home, and they help me sort through the books that have been donated. We then level them by grade and interest level and shelve them on the correct shelf. Then, when I go to a school or donate books to another organization for redistribution, I can easily place certain grade levels of books in the boxes. I have partnered with the local group Seeds of Caring and talked with children and their parents about Books For Bedtime. Families then helped stamp and sort books, including some children only two years old! I have met people who are part of service fraternities from a local university, as well as employees from some wonderfully service-minded businesses, including Victoria Secret, Nationwide Insurance and Cardinal Health, and other charities, such as Ohio Reading Corps.

Books For Bedtime has taught me how kind the world can be; everyone helping me help others has changed my outlook on the world for sure! I now am able to understand that while the world has some bad people in it, most people are good and most people want to help others, much like the Books For Bedtime fans and followers do. My hope is that Books For Bedtime can continue for a long time to come! The smile that I see when a little girl picks out the perfect book is worth every hour of time that I put into Books For Bedtime. That, of course, is my ultimate goal: to get books into the hands of children who need them. I am so proud that over 86,000 books have been given new homes. I am hoping, that in some small way, I am helping to decrease the book deserts that plague our earth.

Abby Diuble
Youth Chair, Cofounder of
Diuble Family Vision Foundation

ABOUT
ABBY DIUBLE

Abigail Diuble lives with her parents and older sister in Manchester, Michigan where she attends Manchester High School. She is the 2022 class president. When she isn't doing service activities, Abigail enjoys spending time at the lake in northern Michigan. She loves animals and children.

I am the younger of two sisters. This story is about me, Abby; however, my story cannot begin without an introduction to my sister, Lilly.

Lilly is two years older than me. She was born with a hearing loss and also has low vision. Lilly's condition will not improve. Her doctors believe her condition will worsen such that she will eventually be blind and deaf. There is currently no treatment or cure for the disease that affects her. At a young age, Lilly became an advocate for those with blinding eye diseases. She began raising money for Foundation Fighting Blindness to fund research to find cures for diseases like the one affecting her. My whole family became involved. She has been a spokesperson for FFB and a youth representative on the board since she was seven years old.

As a result of Lilly's involvement with FFB, I too have been involved. I accompanied my sister and my family to more charitable events than I can count. Stewardship, advocacy, and charitable contribution was and is just a normal way of life for me and my family.

I too have served as a youth representative on the board for FFB. I too have raised money for FFB to fund research. I too have been a spokesperson for advocacy. I've been involved in FFB since the age of five. Together, my sister, my family, and I have raised $200,000 for FFB!

I don't want to say our lives were totally focused on FFB, but it really was just something we always had on our mind. The reality was that my sister was going blind, and we didn't know what else to do aside from raising money for research that may one day lead to a cure for her. We didn't know it, but our lives were about to change.

In late June 2015, my parents and my sister were preparing for a trip to Boston. My mother was to receive an award at an event for FFB. I was not to attend, so I was staying with my grandparents in Northern Michigan. On a hot and sticky Monday night, a tornado struck and severely damaged our home at 1:30 a.m.

My sister does not wear her hearing aids to bed which made her very difficult to awaken. Precious seconds were wasted and, as a result, my mother and sister barely avoided harm. They just made it to the basement stairway as the tornado struck. Where they had been standing literally one second prior was destroyed. One second could have meant the difference between life and death. One second. It was overwhelming for me. I felt helpless. My whole family could have been killed and I wasn't there to help, and when I thought about it, I couldn't have done anything anyway.

I am a doer. I am an advocate. I uphold what is right. How could I be helpless? I was only ten years old at the time, but it was still a very unusual and uncomfortable feeling for me. My home was destroyed. We were trying to find somewhere to live while it would be repaired. All of my personal belongings were either ruined or just gone. And yet, I could not stop thinking about how vulnerable my family was in this emergency situation. I needed to do something. I realized that children like Lilly, with hearing loss or vision loss, really are vulnerable in emergency situations. Of course, we had smoke and carbon monoxide detectors, and we have an emergency plan for fire but never even thought of an emergency plan for a tornado. So, despite that we didn't have a place to live or any of our things, I began to discuss my concerns with my mom. I kept telling her that we needed to help kids like Lilly. She kept saying that right now we needed to help ourselves. That didn't work for me, so I continued to bring it up—a lot.

Finally, we found a house to rent and got sort of settled. We had our beat-up computer on a card table, and I got to work researching different alarm systems that could wake a deaf or hard of hearing sleeper. I found one that I liked because it also connected to a weather alarm. And, of course, weather is what caused our current problematic situation. My mom contacted the manufacturer and we came up with a deal to buy the alarms in bulk for a reduced price. The owners of the company are deaf and were sympathetic to our cause.

I decided that I wanted every hearing-impaired child to have one of these alarms. I called my project WHIP which stands for Warning Hearing Impaired People. I realized that I would need help with this plan. My first thought was that maybe the fire department would be able to help me. I began talking to local fire departments to pitch my idea. The overall consensus was that this was a great idea and that they would help if they could. Now I needed money to purchase the alarms. I tried to apply for grants, but soon realized that I needed to be part of a charitable foundation to do that. I would not be deterred. We began the process to start our own nonprofit immediately. In the meantime, we held a fundraising event to get our finances going. We raised enough to purchase a few alarms.

The nonprofit, Diuble Family Vision, was founded one year after the tornado, and ironically, we gave away our first alarm system to a young boy with a cochlear implant on the anniversary of the tornado!

To date, I have dispensed forty alarm systems to hearing-impaired children. My biggest obstacle with distribution is access. It is hard for me to find out which children need them because of privacy issues with schools. I have started working with our local intermediate school districts to have them disseminate the information and ultimately have the families contact me; however, this is a slow process.

I now do speaking engagements to tell my family's story and to raise awareness for emergency plans for vulnerable children. If just one life is saved by my work, it will make me happy.

My sister and I continue to contribute to Foundation Fighting Blindness. Through our nonprofit, we make yearly donations to FFB to fund research to find cures for blinding eye diseases. We continue to apply for grants and have received several. Lilly and I have been recognized for our community service with several high-profile awards that also have given a grant to our nonprofit.

We feel that advocacy, service, and charity are so important that we have started a scholarship at our high school based on service. We want our work to continue and thought it would be a great way to get others involved. Additionally, we are sponsoring a tenth-grade student in a leadership program in our state. My sister and I have brought a Leos club (Lions Club for kids) to our high school; we serve as president and vice president. The Leos do service projects every month. I feel strongly that we need to build a community of young people that believe service to others is of value.

Helping people is my passion; it is a great feeling to know that I am making a difference in the lives of others. There is so much that young people can do to make the world a better place. I think that they just don't know where to start. I'm excited and happy when I can help others come up with a starting point. I try to live my life as an example that other children would want to follow. In addition to my work with FFB and Diuble Family Vision, I have donated my hair twice to make wigs for children with health problems, I am involved in 4-H, I volunteer at my church, I work at a day care, and I am my high school class president. I am youth cochair for the FFB Michigan VisonWalk and, of course, my family nonprofit, Diuble Family Vision. I have won the Presidential Service Award, Michigan Governor's Service Award, the Prudential Spirit of Community Award, Lions Club International Young Leaders in Service Gold Award, and the Power of Children Award from the Children's Museum of Indianapolis.

With every award or recognition I've receive, I have hoped that other kids would be inspired to do good work in their community. At the Power of Children Awards, I was fortunate to be able to lead a group of children at a symposium on service volunteerism. It was a great feeling to be able to guide other children with their ideas and help them realize that they too can do great things.

I really believe that kids can make a difference in their community and their world. They just need to know that they can.

YOUNG DIVAS THAT CARE

I am so happy to be a guiding force for them. Without my drive to help others, I could have just been a victim of a natural disaster. Instead, my life of service has been instrumental in making me feel empowered. I'm not a victim. I am a vehicle for change. I'm so proud of that, and I want other children to be able to take charge of their bad situations and their lives and help themselves while helping others.

Zoya Surani

Cofounder of Project iConquer,
Singer and Volunteer
at many societies

ABOUT ZOYA SURANI

Zoya Surani is a freshman at Harvard University who plans to major in human developmental and regenerative biology while fulfilling her premed requirements to pursue a career as a neonatologist. Her passions include the life sciences, children, and service. In her free time, apart from working on developments in her nonprofit organization, iConquer: Ubuntu, to bring the nutrition and health curriculum combating obesity and diabetes to children worldwide, she conducts CPR/AED/First Aid certification courses as a Red Cross instructor, serves as a Project Sunshine volunteer director at Tufts Floating Hospital, prepares for Camp Kesem as a counselor, and also works as a tour guide at the Peabody Museum of Archaeology and Ethnology. Her role model is Irena Sendler, a Polish nurse who smuggled Jewish children out of the concentration camps during World War Two. She hopes to make an impact on the world by saving children through neonatology.

When I was five, I started collecting rocks—I would pick them up at playgrounds and carry them home in the soles of my shoes. Each of my rocks have a different color, texture, and memory. I painted a misshaped green flower on a smooth brown rock on my first day of kindergarten. My older sister Sara gave me a sparkly purple geode on my eighth birthday. I was rolling a tiny rigid blue rock between my fingers the day my hometown was declared "The Fattest City in America" and a similar black rock the day my elder sister, Saherish, lost her hearing. I never knew much about rocks. I just liked having an abundance of them associated with the good and bad—a marker for a memory.

The last two memories I stated above were two of the most impactful in my life. Though I had not realized they were similar when they occurred, I realize now how similar they were. Let us first start from the beginning.

It was 2010 and I was freshly ten years old. The news channel was often the background noise as my family ate dinner, but that day, my family's eyes were all glued to the news headline claiming that my city, Corpus Christi, Texas, was named "The Fattest City in America" according to a Men's Health article. While "obesity" and "diabetes" were fairly common terms tossed around in my household, I had never understood the implications behind them. I put down the blue rock I was rolling over with my fingers and listened to Saherish explain how her friend has diabetes. I started playing back memories in my head: *my uncle has diabetes, my friend is at risk for type 2 diabetes because of her weight, my father has obesity.* These realizations started spiraling in my head, and I knew my sisters were on the same page as me. We wanted to do something but did not know where to begin.

As a poet and pianist, I knew music was the first stepping stone. Rather than writing about my own feelings about religion or politics, I wrote instead about my community and this issue. My internal thoughts of what could I do about it and how could I make it my mission to get my city fit were eventually written onto a page, combined with a rhyme scheme, and turned into a song. With help from community members and a rising star Hollywood musician who took a chance on my musings, I launched my first song: "Conquered."

After the release of "Conquered," my sisters and I decided that we could do more than release a song—we could start an educational program! After designing puppet shows, animated movies, whimsical dance routines, catchy jingles, arts and crafts projects, and a giant monkey-bear mascot costume, we launched iConquer. We worked with community members, grant donors, government officials, and educators to teach our iConquer program to more than thirty-five schools in the region. Throughout middle and high school, I strived to make "creating healthy habits" the new rock collecting and have reached more than 15,000 wide-eyed five-year-olds to date.

Regardless of iConquer's successes, in 2016, after finding the perfect black rock and admiring it in the doctor's waiting room, I learned that Saherish had sudden sensorineural hearing loss. After my initial inability to accept the situation, I quickly found the ability to understand Saherish's deafness and open my mind to the needs of other individuals with disabilities. I realized that even though iConquer was reaching disenfranchised populations of South Texas, it was not touching the special needs community.

After contacting local media outlets, universities, and school districts, and as more hands around the community came together, I was reminded of an African tale about children who came together to share a basket of goodies an anthropologist had brought: rather than one child going to claim the basket himself, they all went together. As they came together, they said, "Ubuntu: I am because we are," showing how the only way to progress into the future is if it is done together. Remembering this story, I knew that this new all-inclusive agenda where we would have our curriculum available in braille and

ASL so that all children would be taught side by side, together, must be named iConquer: Ubuntu.

Just as my hometown had been labeled in a negative way, my sister's sudden hearing loss brought her a label that she also did not choose. The rocks I found—blue commonly seen as the color of sorrow and black commonly associated with fear or evil—I had to find beauty in. These rocks kept me grounded and reminded me that who we are is not a constant that can be taken for granted but an always changing, always growing part of this world. There is beauty in everything, whether it be obvious or hidden, and when something labels it elsewise, that just means more has to be done to polish it.

With every rock I placed into my rock tumbler or each individual letter I punched into the braille label maker to transfer onto our published storybook, I knew that slowly, but surely, I was conquering all of the rocks thrown my way.

POEM

What if you woke up one day unable to hear?
How would you feel? Confused, in fear?
You'd be immediately given a new label,
Disabled.
You'd be asked how it happened,
but would lack the answers.
You ask the professionals
for a solution on the matter,
But all they can say is you need an MRI,
Only then could they figure out
what happened, or at least try.
Next, the MRI comes out perfectly normal,
But this is the one time you'd prayed for abnormal.
Had there been an obstruction
they could've removed that,

CANDACE GISH

Restoring your hearing, and
bringing your old self back.
However, there was nothing there,
So now a hearing aid is what you must wear.
How is it that you woke up one day
without hearing in your right ear,
And now disabled is a label you'll wear for years?
This world is a mystery in how it gives and takes,
Leaving you sometimes with happiness,
other times with pain.
Having something taken away makes you miss it
And wish for the day you'll once again have it.
Hearing is not a toy you'll miss,
But something you'll forever wish
To come back to you again,
But with so many unknowns,
it's not sure if it will or when.
The biggest lesson my sister taught me was
to treasure what I have,
And to treasure it again, on her behalf.
She also taught me to recognize individuals for who
they are and not what they lack,
And to do my all to help them feel whole
and give back.
Though it has been over two years since
she lost her hearing,
I will always be there for her and
others like her, cheering.

Danielle Rothchild
President of
Danielle Cares for Chairs,
Chapter President for FCCLA

ABOUT
DANIELLE ROTHCHILD

Danielle Rothchild, eighteen, is a college freshman at Purdue University. She created her own nonprofit at sixteen years old. She collects plastic bread tags, recycles them, and uses the proceeds to buy mobility products. She currently has collected over two million bread tags and has given away six products.

The sizzling sounds of the greasy fryer from cooking the juicy hamburgers and fries at the fast food chain is what sparked an idea that changed my life. With all the food consumed a lot of "trash" is thrown away. While in line ordering my food, I saw a counter full of bread, and looking closer, I saw these tiny plastic squares. These squares are called bread tags, which are recyclable, and billions are wasted each year. I was a member of a career technical student organization in high school called Family Career and Community Leaders of America (FCCLA). This is an amazing organization which helps young adults develop great leadership skills and family values. Every year they have competitive events. I loved competing in the Recycle and Redesign category. I needed to take a product and make it into something else. The bread tags spearheaded the idea to make my dress out of bread tags for the competition.

As my vision of the dress developed, I knew I needed thousands of bread tags. Therefore, I rushed to many restaurants, hospitals, hotels, events, and contacted the headquarters of bread tags to collect. It was intimidating for a sixteen-year-old to communicate with all these big businesses, but it ended up teaching me valuable life lessons. Some businesses were not accommodating to this idea, because there were no benefits for them. Others wondered how a "little girl" could collect enough to be successful. These criticisms did not stop me but made me work harder. As I talked to businesses asking for help, I learned how to handle rejections and how to follow through. I discovered that one needs to be visible and create relationships to be successful. Once I accumulated 40,000 bread tags, I created a 1920s style flapper dress and competed in the event. I won a gold medal and advanced to the national competition where I also received a gold. After that was completed, I decided to continue collecting and help the environment. I researched about bread tags and found a foundation in South Africa called Bread Tags for Wheelchairs. My focus went from making my dress into something much bigger, leading to my foundation Danielle Cares for Chairs.

Bread Tags for Wheelchairs is run by an eighty-year-old woman who collects bread tags and brings them to a recycling plant. In exchange, the recycling plant pays her, which she then buys wheelchairs for people in need. I was very intrigued by this concept where I wanted to continue this eighty-year-old's legacy by starting it in the U.S. I contacted the organization in South Africa and had several Skype meetings. It was mutually decided that we were going to bring this concept to North America. My inspiration was that if an eighty-year-old lady could do this, so could a sixteen-year-old girl. I then researched and located one of the recycling plants that takes the number six polystyrene (bread tags), and lucky for me it happened to be local. I sent the company an e-mail stating what I was doing and asked for their business. I patiently waited for them to respond, and a few days later they did. We met and negotiated a rate per pound of bread tags. A few months later in April of 2017, I was approved to be an official 501(c)3.

It has been an amazing ride starting this organization. Who would have thought that just a few years ago I was a typical shy teen? I struggled in school with having a learning disability and hearing impairment which produced a speech impediment. This left me very self-conscious. I decided when I started high school I could either sit back and let these disabilities define me on who I was or embrace them and move forward. The reality is that having ADD sometimes is a blessing because it allows me to be creative. I believe that my disabilities are not liabilities as much as they are assets. I became a proadvocate for my Individual Education Program which allows me accommodations for some of the skills I was lacking. I actually joined a TV program at school to help me overcome my speech impediment which eventually allowed me to become one of their staff members. I have met with politicians and policy makers to speak about the importance of providing opportunities for students with disabilities and to maintain technical education programs for those who will not have the skills to succeed with heavily based

STEM (science, technical, engineering, and math) curriculums of today's school systems. I also joined a student technical program called Family and Career Community Leaders of America which addresses important personal, family, work, and societal issues. This organization gave me the confidence to become the president of my local chapter and one of ten state officers for Indiana. It also was the stepping stone for me to develop my foundation.

Since the inception of my organization, I have collected over two million bread tags and have given away over six mobility products including four specially adapted power wheel cars and two wheelchairs. We have collection points all around North America, including schools, hospitals and national parks. I have attempted a world record with the longest bread tag chain along with being recognized by Disney/YSA youth award, my local sports teams, and Peace First and featured in a national children's magazine as well as a national TV program. My dresses have been featured at museums and art galleries, and my bread tags have been on display at the library for children to see what one million looks like. More importantly, with all of these accolades I am also proud to admit to facing multiple failures. I am nineteen years old and realize that it is OK to fail at some things because it teaches you how to regroup and try other methods to accomplish your goals. If you believe in something, do the research, and feel that it will succeed, it will. You just have to be prepared to work harder than you may have anticipated. When I first started collecting bread tags, I was told by many people that no one can collect enough to make a dress. That only fueled my fire, and if I just gave up, I never would have experienced all of these opportunities the past few years.

As a global community we are facing an enormous problem with plastic disposal and the limitations of recycling and the impacts the disposal is having on our environment. I was just one little girl, who came up with an idea of how I could make a difference. I took an item that was destined for a landfill, or even worse litter, and created value. I took this value and used it to help our community. Collectively, if we can find others that are willing to come up with similar ideas, we can build a better world for our future.

My goal for the future is to further my education and run this while in college, to spread my message. It may be challenging to be successful, but if an eighty-year-old woman can do it, so can I. Lastly, don't let anyone dull your sparkle, and CHAIRish your bread tags everyone!

Jocelyn Marencik
Founder of GNAT,
A Technology News and
Opportunity Hub for Girls

ABOUT JOCELYN MARENCIK

Jocelyn Marencik is a senior in the Center for Information Technology at Deep Run High School in Glen Allen, Virginia. She is the founder and project manager of a community initiative called Got Tec Richmond. She is also the founder of GNAT, a technology news and opportunity hub for girls.

Since elementary school I have always been involved in community service. In fourth grade in 2011, I started collecting nonperishable goods for the Henrico Christmas Mother Project, benefitting the Central Virginia Food Bank, and still am involved annually. In total, I have donated over 8,000 canned goods to this organization. In middle school I taught myself to crochet and started donating handmade items to the From the Heart Stitchers organization which donates crocheted and knitted items to cancer patients, homeless persons, and veterans. I still donate annually to this cause as well and have crocheted a total of 1,480 hours to date of crocheted hats, scarves, and blankets.

My involvement in community service was taken to a higher level during my freshman year of high school when I combined my passion for computer science and technology with trying to assist and solve a noted educational inequality in area schools. A major issue currently exists in schools with computer science, as not everyone has equal access to technology equipment and learning experiences. Computers are now a part of almost every job and knowing how to use and code computers is essential to an individual's future educational and career success. I noted this issue locally in the Richmond, Virginia area when observing the equipment and classes that more affluent suburban students had access to, as opposed to the lack of the same for the poorer inner city students. This inspired me to found a community initiative known as Got Tec Richmond.

Got Tec, which is an acronym for Gifts of Technology for Teachers, Education, and Children, has a mission of funding and delivering needed technology equipment for underserved schools in Richmond. This includes organizing and mentoring Learn-to-Code or Digital Art-based advocacy events. Most of the students at the schools that my initiative donates to are from low-income families and do not otherwise have access to technology equipment or any previous coding experience. With just a small amount of guidance and encouragement, these students collaborate to program solutions to simple problems or design digital artwork which they excitedly share with their peers. An online coding video library has also been established for students to use for continued learning after the initial events.

I am proud of the measurable impact of Got Tec, which includes over thirty thousand dollars worth of donated equipment, over eighty schools and 120 classrooms served, and over two thousand students directly affected. My initiative has received the Prudential Spirit of Community Virginia State Award, the She++ Include Award, and a CSTA Code.org Champion for Computer Science Student Award. However, these accomplishments do not reflect the most significant outcomes of the initiative, which are giving the students the opportunity to experience a new universal language and potentially helping them find their equal, creative voices through coding. This can be measured in the reactions of the students, including newfound confidence, joy, and a passion for learning something inspiring.

Got Tec has also provided personal growth in several ways. I have learned to better communicate, collaborate, fundraise, and mentor from my initiative. I have listened to the perspectives of and shared ideas with educators, fellow tech enthusiasts, vendors, and supporters. The biggest lesson learned, however, was from the determination, enthusiasm, and curiosity of the disadvantaged students. It's been a most valuable and rewarding experience. I now consider Got Tec an ongoing project that will grow with me as life continues, and I desire to find a school and a community where I can replicate its mission. When you can combine your volunteerism with your passion, it is life-changing for you and for those you've helped.

Libby Hawboldt
Writer, Activist, and Dog Trainer

ABOUT
LIBBY HAWBOLDT

Libby Hawboldt is a fifteen-year-old student living in Alberta. She can be found reading any book she gets her hands on, writing short stories, or attempting to write a novel. Writing has been an outlet for her as she has faced some family challenges like addiction with the help of her family that has raised her since she was two. Having five siblings can be tough, but she finds comfort in her three dogs—Molly, Maple, and Ginny.

I sat on the swing on our porch, the sun just licking the sky, rising to greet me in the morning. The chirping of some bird could be heard in the direction of our big birch tree, but the sound of a joyful family dominated my attention. A sudden happiness filled me up to the brim of my body. The voices of my sibling waking up to a breakfast made by our mom, the sizzling of eggs and some sort of meat could be smelled from the porch. I smiled.

My eyes closed as I enjoyed the peace, knowing I was safe, knowing nothing could hurt me.

TWO MONTHS BEFORE...

I sat on the couch in the living room, my eyes glued to my phone, scrolling through Pinterest. I had just recently got it, Pinterest. A voice from the kitchen told me to go do laundry. I stood up, dragging myself toward the downstairs, my legs and arms felt limp like noodles.

I ran down the stairs skipping two at a time, ignoring a rag on the bottom stair, but my mind kept on falling back to a pin I had just read. It was about a girl whose dad had left her on the streets as a baby. A sad feeling ran along my veins, sending my mind into a state of sadness. Just like a father I knew, a father who preferred alcohol and this world's desires over his own daughter.

After I finished the laundry, this gloomy feeling didn't leave me for the rest of the day, and I started to realize the simple things in life that made me feel this same gloomy feeling.

A WEEK LATER

My stomach hurt, a rumbling sound exploded from my belly, but I didn't care. It was inside my chest that truly hurt, and I didn't know why. I held my fingers to my eyes, tears welling up, soon to fall. *What was wrong with me?* Why was I feeling like this; why was I crying? I wasn't sad or anything. I was completely perfect. Nothing was wrong; nothing could be... So why should I tell anyone about this stupid pain?

TWO WEEKS LATER

I walked to my room, a smile running along my face. A fake happiness, a mask, an act. I slowly opened my door, shutting it after I was inside my room.

I slide against the door, falling on to the ground. The carpet rubbing alongside my skin, making my legs and fingers tingle. I didn't need to see the tears. I knew they were streaming down my face, my cheeks, my neck, my useless body.

I felt like I was drowning in my tears and I couldn't scream or yell. All I wanted was to be free, to feel happy, to be happy.

My crying was silent, like every other time I seemed to find myself in this low state. This state of unworthiness, grief, misery, unhappiness.

I couldn't keep it inside for long, that's the one upsetting thing about not letting anyone see your true feelings, bottling them up, they had to be released sometime.

I held a blade in my hand. I had to smash my razer repeatedly to get this. I had found this idea on Pinterest. And for what? So I could cut? I didn't even know if this would work. If cutting would let me have some control over the pain. But I guess if it meant the pain would be felt on my skin and not in my heart, I was willing to do it, to self harm. I took in a deep breath, my teeth chattering, willing the blade to slide along my skin.

A throbbing pain shot through my leg as blood started to gush from my scratch. I felt like screaming. Not because of the pain, because of the reason why I was cutting. No one deserved to feel like this, not a single soul, but here I was, feeling this horrible way.

Life wasn't fair. I knew that for a fact, but just because something isn't fair doesn't mean you shouldn't try to make as many things as you can to be fair. And this one thing, me feeling like a waste of space, wasn't fair. It truly wasn't. What had I done to deserve this? Nothing. But I was still here slicing away at my own skin.

A single tear ran down my face. It dropped down onto my fresh cut. Mixing with the blood, causing it to turn a dark pink.

My hand was shaking. I set down my blade, not wanting to bleed too much, hoping it wouldn't bleed through my jeans. I was praying that no one would ever find out about anything that happened inside my mind, the thoughts like poison, seeping through my brain causing me to do these terrible things, causing my life to fall apart.

I just wanted to find a way to fix it, to find the broken pieces and glue them back together. But I didn't have glue and I couldn't figure out how to fix everything. I knew these feelings wouldn't go away. I had to look perfect. They just all had to believe that I was perfect. I just had to fool them.

When I was alone, then I could be my true self, the imperfect broken self, the girl I had to see each day, the girl that wanted to cut. I wept, and covering my face with a towel, I tried to catch my tears.

A knock on the door brought me out of my state of sadness. I cleared my throat.

"Almost done." I said this in a casual voice.

"OK, Mom wants you." I hid my face in my towel. Every time I had to talk to or see my parents my stomach ached. I got so nervous that maybe somehow, they found out.

Two weeks later

I dug my nails into my skin, mind running wild. I had just put on my bathing suit and scars ran all along my upper thigh. I gasped. I didn't think it would look this bad.

There was no way someone wouldn't notice them. They stood out like diamonds in a sea of rocks, shining like a lighthouse over a sky of darkness. My heart raced in my chest, and my breath came out in fast short gasps.

This wasn't happening. It couldn't happen, not now. I couldn't let them see. I took a few bandages and stuck them to my scars. It didn't look natural, and I would have to explain why I had bandages on my legs. I ripped each one off very carefully, trying not to bleed. Trying not to be seen, by the blind eyes of a mother, a mother who fell for an act so easily.

It hurt to think about it, how I could fool so many people I loved, to catch them unawares. They couldn't see past a mask I wore, a mask hiding me behind a wall I was building. A wall that kept me from getting hurt, from being seen. I dug through my drawers searching for shorts. I eventually found a pair of all-black shorts.

I put them on. As I predicted, they worked perfect—no blood spots were seen. I smiled, a rare thing. It had worked. I could stay hidden, invisible, a thing I was way too good at.

ONE WEEK LATER

I sat in my room, my iPad sitting in my lap. I scrolled through random pins, saving them to different boards. One pin stuck out to me, a pin explaining how suicide made people feel, how they were struggling and felt trapped in their bodies. I saved it to my board called "Me." I knew most of my boards were private.

So I never suspected anyone to see it.

Two hours later I opened my iPad, and going to Pinterest, two notifications popped up. I immediately clicked them. My heart stopped for a second. Two of my friends had texted me. One asked what this was and why I was posting suicidal pins. Another asked for my parent's number, but I knew she had seen the pin. She had never asked for my number in my life. Two years I had known her and she barley talked to me.

I covered my mouth, knowing they wanted to tell my parents, knowing they would find out. My insides hurt, my lungs were gasping for air, I couldn't breathe properly, my mind and lungs hurt like fire was set ablaze inside me.

I took a pillow to my face and screamed, letting my anger stream into the pillow. My heart was filled with fear. If they found out they would hate me, they would ask why, and they would finally see who I really was.

Me and my sister went outside for our paper route, delivering papers to every house; I let my mind slip from my body. Not wanting to think, to feel, to breathe. If only I had some way to do it, to end it all here. How was I going to be happy in a world of pain, in a world trying to kill me?

Nothing but trouble arose from the sea I called my mind. Thoughts of worry bubbled out in every turn of the maze I called my brain.

I had to face them, to take what I deserved. Most likely they would cry or make me feel bad. I didn't want any of this. I didn't need any of this. On top of a mountain of worries laid my parents, their faces looking down at me with disgust. I was the problem the reason for their pain.

I wanted to scream, to yell, to smash anything in site. To fly away from this world.

Over time, I finally had to face my parents. And it wasn't pretty.

Once we had figured out everything, my parents had taken every razer in the house and hid them somewhere. They even had me go to a counselor. I never thought telling them, explaining, could be so easy—how simple it was, like admitting that I had somewhere to go. Yes, the words got stuck in my throat, but they eventually came out.

Nothing but faded scars—that's what my suicidal thoughts had turned into. An ugly thing from the past. Gratefully, the scars on my wrists had blended into my skin till they were almost invisible, but the damage was still in my head. I never could joke around about death ever again. Just the simplest joke like "I'm dead" made me feel weird and uncomfortable, and my parents didn't trust me with razors for a while.

But still, it was better than being dead. I had gotten through one of the hardest times in my life, a time of darkness and fear. But how?

Well there were three things to keep in mind. One, never try to do things on your own. It's OK to be independent but not to the point where you don't ask anyone for help. That's not good, or healthy. It can get to the point where you seclude yourself away from the world and that's how problems begin, not letting anyone help you. If things get out of hand talk to someone. It's better than being sad or depressed. As for me personally, I gave it to God. He was the one there the whole time. Telling your parents may feel like the end of the world, but if you don't, it may be your end. There is so much to live for and you are worth it.

Two, never fear the results of telling someone. Who cares if they get mad or angry. If they truly love you they won't judge or hate you.

Three, no matter what look at the bright and wonderful things in life, enjoy your life, and cherish every moment on earth. It could be gone like that. Never focus on just the bad. If you do, it's not going to fix anything.

Don't let the past dominate the present. No matter what you've gone through or what you're going through, give it to God and just remember to learn from the past. Live in the now and plan for the future.

Calla Legue

ABOUT CALLA LEGUE

Calla Legue is a paramedic student, a dog mom, an athlete, and a changemaker. Her goal is to make a difference in people's lives, whether it be listening to someone talk about their day or to literally provide CPR in an attempt to save a life. She was a volunteer at the 2018 Ottawa Pride and is a big supporter of the LGBTQ community.

In life you're always given the bad or given the good, and it all depends on how you're going to view it in order to deal with it and continue on with your life. Growing up, I was faced with a lot of challenges that forced me to grow up quicker than I should have, but these challenges have also shaped me to be the person I am today. My father was an alcoholic who in order to express his love would buy things unexpectedly with money we certainly didn't have. When he would drink you never would know what kind of mood he would be in; either happy and fun, the best person to be around, or the sad, depressed, violent, and angry man. Even the nights where he was happy and fun would lead to violence and anger. Then, life decided to give me a brother who was heavily into drugs and was also very violent toward me. Yes, every brother and sister fight but these fights left physical and mental scars that will never be forgotten. Life gave me an amazing mother; life knew I needed a small break sometimes. However, it was not always easy. Many times, I begged for my mom to leave my dad after nights of drinking, after seeing him push her around and yell at her, after watching my mom cry for days. My mom and I certainly did not have a strong relationship but over the years developed into a strong mother and daughter relationship.

Throughout my childhood I have seen and experienced things that made me question myself a lot. I was always feeling scared, lost, and alone. I would take matters into my own hands and didn't cope properly, leaving me with long lasting scars. But occasionally life would throw me some good things like a new puppy or dad not drinking for a while, but sure enough this good would only last so long, throwing ten times more bad at me. With this constant state of uneasiness, or not feeling like I belonged, I was given an out. When I was thirteen I was asked to go to camp at the Tim Horton Children Foundation, where I was able to truly discover my best. Here I felt free. I was able to talk to people who made me feel comfortable, who allowed me to express myself, who made me the person I am today. The following year I had the pleasure of returning to camp for the

Youth Leadership program for the next five years. During these five years I learned many leadership skills, met long lasting friends, and continued to find the person I wanted to be. Camp allowed me to branch off and experience new things, giving me hope and guiding me to a positive path. Camp is home away from home. You did well life, for giving me this great thing.

As time went on, things were slowly starting to get better. My family dynamic had changed greatly, my relationship with my mom had improved, I was doing well with school, and I felt comfortable with the person I was becoming. Because of my hardships I have been dealt with, I knew I wanted to help people and help prevent children from going through similar situations that I did. I knew I wanted to make a difference and work within my abilities to impact people in any way possible. So I decided to go to school for social work as a way to give back to all those who helped guide me. However, during my postsecondary education I wasn't enjoying the program and felt like I didn't belong, so I switched into a program called Health Promotion which further lead me into the paramedic program where I am today. This program and further occupation allows me to use my mental and physical abilities but also allows me to impact someone's life by showing trust and empathy. Here I feel as though I belong.

But before entering this program I was still feeling lost. I knew that I was in such a great place in life, and I knew I wanted to make a difference but I felt as though I wasn't succeeding. Since I was a camper myself at the Tim Horton Children Foundation, I knew I wanted to work there after I was no longer a camper. So I got the pleasure to work in Manitoba, where I was able to further branch off and travel more than I had ever imagined. During this experience, I was given a few campers that gave me a hard time behavioral wise, but I always knew ways around it and worked together with them one-on-one. But there was one challenging camper who I will never forget. She's not unforgettable because she was so bad, but because she was so hurt and unloved that she was used to acting this way and didn't know how to change. She was very stubborn and unhappy, kept to herself, and wouldn't listen. I spent some time with this camper, and she felt comfortable enough with me to share what she was going through at home. It broke my heart knowing what life decided to give her but ensured her that she is loved and that she is important.

On the last day of camp before sending her home, she set up a scavenger hunt for me with little clues leading to a letter. The leader read:

> Tetris,
>
> Thank you so much for everything. I've never been able to express myself to my mom like I did with you. You're like the mom that I never had, you have changed my life so much and I have no idea how to thank you.
>
> Sorry for being stubborn, but I grew up learning not to trust, but because of you I can trust again. So thank you so much for being my hero and not giving up on me when I did. Thank you for the hugs and everything.
>
> I'll miss you so much

This will forever hold a special place in my heart, knowing that I did this, I made someone feel as though they are loved and taught them that they can trust. I was part of the good that life decided to give her. Actually, knowing that I impacted someone's life like this reassured me that I was succeeding in making a difference.

Despite everything that I have been through, it's an amazing feeling to look back and think, "Wow, I overcome that. I am here now. I have done what I've done. I am who I am." Life is not meant to be easy, but it's not always going to be hard. Surround yourself with people who make you happy, who make you feel loved. Some things are out of your control, there's no doubt about that. But you have two ways to look at it: "why is life always giving me so much shit?" or "this sucks, this is hard, here's what I have to do." I can promise you, if you change your perspective when given a challenge, it'll improve how you handle things.

I always say, "*Ces't la vie*," meaning "that's life." I say this because every time I'm given another challenge, I know it's life doing its job by testing my abilities. But I refuse to let life break me down and win. Don't let life win and beat you. I believe in you.

SUBMIT YOUR STORY

Divas That Care is calling for submissions for our next Young Divas That Care book.

We're looking for stories of proactive, passionate young women ages 14—20 that make us feel connected, empowered, and hopeful for the future. If you don't hear from us, please don't take our silence personally. We may be considering your story for a later title. It can take many months or even a few years for a Divas That Care book to be completed. Please be patient as the selection of stories and poems is a time-consuming process. Please do not contact us to ask for an update about your story unless you need to know whether we are considering it because another publisher is interested in it too.

If we choose your story or poem for a future edition of a Divas That Care publication, we will notify you by e-mail and request your permission to print it. We never publish anything without written permission from the author.

If your e-mail address changes after you submit your story, be sure to let our editor know by e-mailing:

submissions@divasthatcare.com

Submit at:
www.divasthatcare.com